FREAKY PHENOMENA

HEALING

FREAKY PHENOMENA

The Series

CONSCIOUSNESS
FAITH
HEALING
LIFE AFTER DEATH
MYSTERIOUS PLACES
PERSONALITY
PSYCHIC ABILITIES
THE SENSES

FREAKY PHENOMENA

HEALING

Don Rauf

Foreword by Joe Nickell, Senior Research Fellow, Committee for Skeptical Inquiry

MASON CREST

Mason Crest
450 Parkway Drive, Suite D Broomall, PA 19008
www.masoncrest.com

Printed in the United States of America

First printing
9 8 7 6 5 4 3 2 1

Series ISBN: 978-1-4222-3772-4
Hardcover ISBN: 978-1-4222-3775-5
ebook ISBN: 978-1-4222-8009-6

Cataloging-in-Publication Data is available on file at the Library of Congress.

Developed and Produced by Print Matters Productions, Inc. (www.printmattersinc.com)
Cover and Interior Design by: Bill Madrid, Madrid Design
Composition by Carling Design

Picture credits: 9, syolacan/iStock; 10, DanBrandenburg/iStock; 12, triocean/Shutterstock; 15, DOUGBERRY/iStock; 17, leezsnow/iStock; 18, Ocskay Bence/Shutterstock; 21, jamesbenet/iStock; 22, Syda Productions/Shutterstock; 23, Samrith Na Lumpoon/Shutterstock; 24, kokouu/iStock; 27, dolgachov/iStock; 29, 7postman/iStock; 30, tjasam/iStock; 32, Krista Kennell/Shutterstock; 32, Dfree/Shutterstock; 32, Everett Collection/Shutterstock; 33, Kerrick/iStock; 34, sdigital/iStock; 35, Stellar-Serbia/iStock; 36, Ezume Images/Shutterstock; 38, Chaikom/Shutterstock; 39, Kaspars Grinvalds/Shutterstock; 41, Alina555/iStock; 42, Savany/iStock

Cover: Nikki Zalewski/Shutterstock

CONTENTS

KEY ICONS TO LOOK FOR:

Words to understand: These words with their easy-to-understand definitions will increase the reader's understanding of the text while building vocabulary skills.

Sidebars. This boxed material within the main text allows readers to build knowledge, gain insights, explore possibilities, and broaden their perspectives by weaving together additional information to provide realistic and holistic perspectives.

Educational Videos: Readers can view videos by scanning our QR codes, providing them with additional educational content to supplement the text. Examples include news coverage, moments in history, speeches, iconic sports moments and much more!

Series glossary of key terms: This back-of-the book glossary contains terminology used throughout this series. Words found here increase the reader's ability to read and comprehend higher-level books and articles in this field.

Advice From a Full-Time Professional Investigator of Strange Mysteries

I wish I'd had books like this when I was young. Like other boys and girls, I was intrigued by ghosts, monsters, and other freaky things. I grew up to become a stage magician and private detective, as well as (among other things) a literary and folklore scholar and a forensic-science writer. By 1995, I was using my varied background as the world's only full-time professional investigator of strange mysteries.

As I travel around the world, lured by its enigmas, I avoid both uncritical belief and outright dismissal. I insist mysteries should be *investigated* with the intent of solving them. That requires *critical thinking*, which begins by asking useful questions. I share three such questions here, applied to brief cases from my own files:

Is a particular story really true?

Consider Louisiana's Myrtles Plantation, supposedly haunted by the ghost of a murderous slave, Chloe. We are told that, as revenge against a cruel master, she poisoned three members of his family. Phenomena that ghost hunters attributed to her spirit included a mysteriously swinging door and unexplained banging noises.

The Discovery TV Channel arranged for me to spend a night there alone. I learned from the local historical society that Chloe never existed and her three alleged victims actually died in a yellow fever epidemic. I prowled the house, discovering that the spooky door was simply hung off center, and that banging noises were easily explained by a loose shutter.

Does a claim involve unnecessary assumptions?

In Flatwoods, WV, in 1952, some boys saw a fiery UFO streak across the evening sky and apparently land on a hill. They went looking for it, joined by others. A flashlight soon revealed a tall creature with shining eyes and a face shaped like the ace of spades. Suddenly, it swooped at them with "terrible claws," making a high-pitched hissing sound. The witnesses fled for their lives.

Half a century later, I talked with elderly residents, examined old newspaper accounts, and did other research. I learned the UFO had been a meteor. Descriptions of the creature almost perfectly matched a barn owl—seemingly tall because it had perched on a tree limb. In contrast, numerous incredible assumptions would be required to argue for a flying saucer and an alien being.

Is the proof as great as the claim?

A Canadian woman sometimes exhibited the crucifixion wounds of Jesus—allegedly produced supernaturally. In 2002, I watched blood stream from her hands and feet and from tiny scalp wounds like those from a crown of thorns.

However, because her wounds were already bleeding, they could have been self-inflicted. The lance wound that pierced Jesus' side was absent, and the supposed nail wounds did not pass through the hands and feet, being only on one side of each. Getting a closer look, I saw that one hand wound was only a small slit, not a large puncture wound. Therefore, this extraordinary claim lacked the extraordinary proof required.

These three questions should prove helpful in approaching claims and tales in Freaky Phenomena. I view the progress of science as a continuing series of solved mysteries. Perhaps you too might consider a career as a science detective. You can get started right here.

Joe Nickell
Senior Research Fellow, Committee for Skeptical Inquiry
Amherst, NY

THE POWER OF POSITIVE THINKING

A s we're often told, health really is one of the most important things in life. Without good health, life can be very hard. Luckily, the body often has a remarkable ability to heal. The body can overcome flu, bones can mend, and wounds can close. Modern medicine has also greatly contributed to keeping us alive and kicking. Research has demonstrated that the power of the mind can also keep bodies sound and help return us to good health.

Can your state of mind really rid you of disease? Stamatis Moraitis believed so. In 1976, Moraitis was living in Florida when he started having shortness of breath. He was diagnosed with terminal lung cancer and given nine months to live. He went for additional opinions and all the doctors told him the same thing—his condition was beyond treatment. He decided to enjoy his remaining time to the fullest. He moved back his native Ikaria, a Greek island where his family had come from. He and his wife moved into a modest home there with his elderly parents. They drank wine, harvested vegetables from the garden, napped, played board games, laughed with friends, and enjoyed the ocean air. His days were worry-free as he savored all the simple pleasures of life. As the months went by, he felt stronger. His breathing eased. After nine months, he was still going strong. Then, years went by. At the 25-year mark, he made a return trip to the United States. He went to revisit with the doctors who had given him the fatal diagnosis. His doctors had all died. Moraitis chalked up his longevity to a contented mind and a happy way of life. He lived until 102.

Throughout history, there are stories like this that demonstrate how the mind can help heal. Sometimes belief is everything and that's why placebos (or fake medicines) can work. Other times, people can relieve stress and anxiety through biofeedback, healing crystals, acupuncture,

hypnosis, and other techniques, and this calming of the mind can greatly benefit their health. This volume of Freaky Phenomena looks at the healing power of the brain, and how nonconventional approaches—outside the realm of normal medicine—can bring healing to some (although success is not always guaranteed).

Tai chi is an ancient Chinese self-healing tradition. Specific postures, breathing techniques, and meditation work to reduce stress and anxiety.

CHAPTER I

BIOFEEDBACK

A biofeedback device placed on the finger uses sensors to read a person's vital statistics.

B iofeedback, sometimes called *neurofeedback*, is a treatment to achieve better health in which you learn to control your body's functions (such as your heart rate) through the use of electrical sensors. The sensors give information (feedback) about your body (bio). Stroke victims have used the process to regain control of muscles. The overstressed have used the technique to relax. Biofeedback has helped people beat insomnia and lower blood pressure. The approach has provided relief for those suffering from migraines and tension headaches, disorders of the digestive system, cardiac arrhythmias (irregularities of the heartbeat), Raynaud's disease (a circulatory disorder that causes uncomfortably cold hands), epilepsy, and paralysis. It has even helped individuals with bladder control problems.

Scientific Take: Hack Your Brain

Biofeedback is a technique of mind over matter. It teaches how to be aware of and manipulate your physical processes to achieve a healthier mind-body state. In the 1960s, biofeedback was just catching on and was often associated with **parapsychology** and Eastern **mystics**. Back then, for some, the idea that you could control your brain waves and that could influence your health seemed farfetched.

Words to Understand

Mindfulness: A meditation practice for bringing one's attention to the internal and external experiences occurring in the present moment.

Mystics: People who have supernatural knowledge or experiences; they have a supposed insight into spirituality and mysteries transcending ordinary human knowledge.

Obsessive compulsive disorder: An anxiety disorder in which people have a pattern of unwanted, repeated thoughts, feelings, ideas, or fears (obsessions) that lead to repetitive behaviors (compulsions).

Parapsychology: Study of paranormal and psychic phenomena considered inexplicable in the world of traditional psychology.

Yoga is one of several ways one can meditate, or practice mindfulness.

Studies since that time have shown it to be effective in some cases, and that even involuntary functions could be controlled by the mind. The fact is, some people seem to be able to will themselves into a healthier state.

The purpose for most biofeedback is to teach people how to relax. Stress can cause or worsen a lot of physical problems—getting rid of the stress can be a cure.

Biofeedback devices vary, but most systems include sensors or electrodes that are placed on the skin or fingers. These sensors can detect changes in heart rate, skin temperature, or muscle tension. For example, in treating high blood pressure, a person may be instructed to relax and take deep, regular breaths until a light on the device comes on, indicating that their blood pressure has gone down.

With some biofeedback systems the user wears a headset or small metal discs are attached to the scalp, and brain waves are measured through an electroencephalogram (EEG), a test that shows electrical activity of the brain. The devices are frequently used to diagnose and monitor epilepsy, seizures, brain diseases, hyperactivity, post-traumatic stress, and other ailments involving the mind.

When meditating (or practicing **mindfulness**), a person using a biofeedback machine can see if he or she is producing brain waves that indicate a relaxed state. Some current devices may present an image that represents calm when this peaceful state is reached. One such device presents an image of an increasingly bright sunrise as the person strives for maximum relaxation. Sometimes therapists run biofeedback sessions, but systems are available for home self-use as well. Affordable systems can plug into laptops, tablets, and smartphones. To achieve a condition of relaxation, individuals might concentrate on specific images or tighten and release certain muscles.

Find out more about biofeedback and the science behind it.

Stopping the Pain from Within

Biofeedback has been used to manage pain for years. Susan Antelis, a mental health counselor, suffered from severe migraines since she was 13. The condition ran in her family. The headaches made her incapable of doing anything. Medications didn't work and by age 20, she had become increasingly depressed and suicidal. She finally turned to biofeedback. Over the course of 10 months, during which she worked to control her temperature readings and muscles with biofeedback, she became almost headache-free.

Getting Better through Games

An architect in Scottsdale, AZ, reported that she was once very successful at her job, but she had developed an **obsessive compulsive disorder** that made her so afraid of germs and contamination that she reached a point where she could not leave her house. She tried a variety of medications, but none helped. She visited a specialist in biofeedback and had her brain measured and mapped. Then the readings of her brain were compared with normal brain waves. Her doctor treated her using specific video games that have been shown to help irregular brain activity. Patients play the game as their brain is monitored. By simply playing these games, the woman's brainwaves returned to normal—she got her disorder under control and returned to work.

In a similar way, there are biofeedback games designed to help teenagers deal with anger issues. A study from Boston Children's Hospital found that a video game that is similar to Space Invaders could help youngsters decrease their anger. In the game, kids shoot at enemy spaceships and leave friendly ones alone. This game is called RAGE (Regulate And Gain Emotional) Control. If a certain indicator rises, showing that they're hyper, players lose the ability to shoot. Two other similar games are Alien Therapy and Angry Heart.

One boy being treated at the University of California, Los Angeles (UCLA) had a severe seizure disorder and was also very disagreeable. He responded poorly to all medications. His

Those with obsessive compulsive disorder can easily lose control. Tasks that appear simple to others—cleaning their hands, washing the dishes—can suddenly take hours or days. Biofeedback has assisted some with this disorder, helping them regain control of their lives.

parents and his doctors thought brain surgery might be the only solution. They decided as a last-ditch effort they would try neurofeedback. After 25 sessions, the boy was seizure-free, and as he continued with the biofeedback his mood improved as well—his parents saw him do something he almost never did: smile. His seizures never returned.

Biofeedback Has Helped
Stroke Patients Bounce Back

After having a stroke in 1995, Dr. Howard Rocket of Toronto, Ontario, had paralysis of his left side. In rehab, a therapist attached an electrode with a metal plate over the bicep muscle of his arm and attached the electrode's wire to a biofeedback system that included a monitor. When Rocket moved that muscle, a line would move up on a graph on the monitor screen. The more he moved the bicep muscle, the higher the line climbed on the graph.

"It was like making a cursor move on a computer screen," he said in an interview on the American Stroke Association (ASA) website.

In biofeedback post-stroke therapy, when the survivor moves the targeted muscle, an electrical signal travels from the electrode on the muscle to the system monitor, where it produces a particular image. The survivor gets reinforcement every time he or she moves the muscle and creates this image. Biofeedback gives a visual cue that the survivor is moving muscles in a desired way. It helps isolate which muscle to use.

On the ASA web site, Dr. Richard L. Harvey, medical director of the Stroke Rehabilitation Center at the Rehabilitation Institute of Chicago, states, "After a stroke, it is common for survivors to move their arms or legs abnormally. Biofeedback can train a survivor to move more naturally."

There are no risks with biofeedback," he adds. "It can train a survivor to open his or her hand by extending the fingers and relaxing the finger flexors. Its main

Beware of Scams

As with many types of medical treatment technology, you have to be careful that a biofeedback machine is truly measuring real biological markers—blood pressure, brain waves, etc. Just because a light turns on, it doesn't necessarily mean a device is working. For example, one man developed and sold a biofeedback machine called the Electro-Physio-Feedback-Xrroid (EPFX) System. The manufacturer said that his equipment could also diagnose and destroy disease. The U.S. Food and Drug Administration eventually indicted the inventor of this biofeedback machine on felony fraud charges and he fled the country. The Seattle Times labeled sales of the EPFX a worldwide scam.

A doctor will apply sensors or electrodes to a patients fingers or skin. Then, the doctor can evaluate the test results.

drawback is it's usually not helpful for learning a functional task like drinking from a cup. So bio-feedback can improve motor control but does not focus on improved functional use."

CHAPTER 2

THE PLACEBO EFFECT

A pill with medication and a pill with
no active ingredient look the same.

A placebo is a medication or therapy that a patient thinks is real but is in fact a fake but harmless treatment. A placebo pill, for example, may contain sugar, starch, or saline but no actual medicine. It can also be a fake injection or "pretend" procedure. Some studies have shown patients make remarkable recoveries when they think they are receiving powerful medicines even if they are "dummy" treatments. Placebos have been shown to lower blood pressure, eliminate warts, stop stomach pain, get rid of headaches, reduce stress, and more.

The *placebo effect* depends on a belief that the mind can improve health. It goes back to ancient cultures. **Shamans** and medicine men or women would perform ceremonies that had no real health benefit, but a belief in their positive effects would often make people feel better. The American Cancer Society (ACS) says that 1 in 3 people experience some sort of positive effect from placebos. On the other hand, many medical groups say that placebos "do not cure." For example, placebos have little if any effect on shrinking a cancerous tumor, according to the ACS. In scientific studies, researchers will compare the effectiveness of a new medication or treatment against a placebo.

Scientific Take: The Power of Belief

In some cases, it appears that when a person believes or expects that a treatment will work, the mind can affect the body's chemistry in a positive way. A patient's expectations and motivations seem to

Words to Understand

Creatine: An organic acid found in muscle tissue and a popular sports supplement used to gain mass.

Endorphins: Hormones secreted within the brain and nervous system that trigger a positive feeling in the body.

Meniscus: A C-shaped piece of tough, rubbery cartilage that works to absorb shock between the shinbone and thighbone.

Shaman: A person believed to have a magic ability to cure.

A documentary about the science and psychology of placebos.

be factors that can positively change their health. This is sometimes called an expectation effect. Scientific evidence suggests that the placebo effect on pain may be partly due to the release of endorphins in the brain. **Endorphins** are the body's natural painkillers. Placebos clearly can help reduce certain symptoms such as pain, anxiety, and trouble sleeping in some people. Scientists say there is also an interesting related "conditioning" effect that shows the power of the placebo. With this effect, if a person is given a medication that works (for example, a pain reliever) and then is given a placebo later that he or she believes is the medication, that person may be better able to tolerate pain.

A Doctor Who "Cured" Cancer with Distilled Water

In 1950, a pilot who was suffering from an advanced cancer of the lymph nodes called *lympho-sarcoma* was desperately searching for a treatment that would help him. All previous therapies had failed. The patient, Mr. Wright, had tumors the size of tennis balls in areas of the neck, groin, chest, and abdomen. His spleen and liver were enlarged. Doctors drained two quarts of milky fluid from his chest every day so he could breathe. Mr. Wright heard about a new experimental drug called Krebiozen. Although the medication wasn't officially approved by the U.S. Food and Drug Administration, Mr. Wright was convinced that the drug would help him. Krebiozen was only being given to patients who were expected to live no longer than three months. Because Mr. Wright fit the criteria, his doctor was able to get him the drug. After receiving the first injection, the tumors reportedly "melted like snowballs on a stove." The drug was nothing short of miraculous. After 10 days, Mr. Wright was declared cancer-free and left the hospital. The pilot was soon back flying again and living a healthy, productive life.

Two months later, scientific reports came out questioning the effectiveness of Krebiozen. The articles deeply depressed Mr. Wright and his tumors returned.

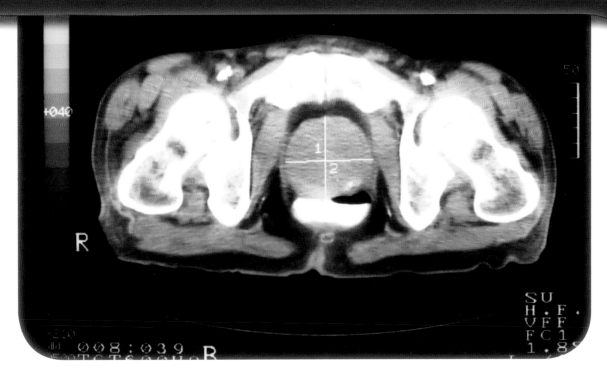

CT scans are used to detect tumors and cancers throughout the body.

His doctor decided to try an experiment. He told Mr. Wright that the initial batch of Krebiozen had been ineffective because it had weakened and lost its potency during shipping. He said he now had a more powerful, ultra-pure version of the drug. Of course, Mr. Wright didn't know that this was all made up, so he eagerly wanted to try the more powerful medication. Instead of receiving any form of Krebiozen, Mr. Wright was given a shot of distilled water. Again, the tumors disappeared, and he felt great.

Shortly thereafter, however, the American Medical Association announced that Krebiozen was not effective at all in treating cancer or any other disease. Krebiozen consisted only of the amino acid **creatine** dissolved in mineral oil. Mr. Wright was devastated by the news. He lost all belief in Krebiozen and died two days later. Years later in 1957, psychologist Bruno Klopfer of UCLA wrote about the case in an article entitled "Psychological Variables in Human Cancer," and the story has become a prime example of how effective a placebo might be.

Even Fake Alcohol Can Make You Drunk

The placebo effect has been demonstrated with non-alcoholic drinks that were presented as real drinks. In a 2003 study out of New Zealand, scientists told a group of students they were being given vodka and tonic to drink when in reality they were being given just tonic. The students acted drunk, and some even showed physical signs of intoxication.

Partygoers have fallen into a drunken state, even after drinking non-alcoholic beverages.

Placebos Can Work Even When You Know

It makes sense that a placebo can work when a person believes he or she is getting real medication. But some studies have shown that a placebo can work even if the person knows it's a sham. In a study out of Harvard University in 2010, researchers gave a placebo to patients suffering from irritable bowel syndrome. They were told that they were going to be given a pill that had no active ingredients and was clearly labeled as a placebo. The patients who took the placebo experienced more relief of symptoms, compared with those who did nothing. Doctors said that by simply performing the medical ritual of taking a pill, the patients seemed to improve—perhaps they felt they were at least doing something to better their condition and this mental change was enough to boost their health.

The Nocebo Effect

There is a darker version of the healing-inducing placebo effect. The *nocebo effect* comes about when a patient is given a placebo, which they believe is a drug that can cause side effects. If a person is warned that the placebo causes nausea, vomiting, fatigue, diarrhea, and other ill effects, he or she may experience those very same symptoms. The worst kind of nocebo effect may be "voodoo death." This is an expression used to describe the phenomenon of a person being told that he or she is going to die and then actually dying. There have been cases where patients were mistakenly told that they only had months to live. Even though these patients had no life-threatening ailment, they died. This is an extreme nocebo effect and shows the power of suggestion.

Even Fake Surgeries Work

Also known as sham surgeries, placebo surgeries are surgeries that are not performed at all. Patients were told they were operated on (for pain, for example) and then they were cured although no operation took place. Several investigations have shown the method to be effective. In a 2014 study, scientists followed a group of patients who had pain from a torn **meniscus**. One set of patients received actual surgery, whereas the other thought they had surgery—doctors went through the motions, making and closing incisions, but not performing any real operation. Afterward, patients who had the fake procedure experienced just as much improvement in pain and activity as those whose meniscus was actually repaired.

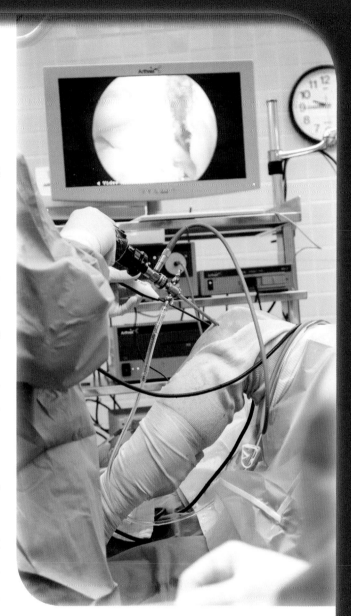

When patients underwent fake surgery, they still received incisions as if they had had the actual procedure.

CHAPTER 3

ACUPUNCTURE

The ancient Chinese medical treatment—acupuncture—has been used for centuries. Although the treatment still has its skeptics, there are many who swear by its benefits.

Acupuncture is an ancient Chinese medical treatment involving the pricking of the skin with hair-thin needles. The therapy is based on the idea that all humans have a life force called *chi* that runs along pathways called *meridians*. When the needles are inserted at different points in your meridians, they influence energy flow. The stimulation from the needles promotes self-healing. The practice has been shown to cure insomnia, help pain, enhance digestion, boost emotional well-being, and improve other ailments. Interest in acupuncture grew in the 1970s after President Nixon visited China. Today, more than three million Americans use acupuncture, according to the National Institutes of Health.

Skeptics believe that acupuncture works in the same way that placebos work—people who believe it works tend to improve. Acupuncturists do not need or usually have an official medical degree, although the therapy is now being used more by general practitioners and physiotherapists.

Scientific Take: A Nervous Reaction?

Although investigators have not found any concrete evidence to prove that humans have a chi or meridians, research has shown that acupuncture actually releases endorphins in the body, and these

Words to Understand

Migraines: Recurring moderate-to-severe throbbing headaches that can last from four hours to three days.

Neurotransmitters: Chemicals released by nerve fibers that transmit signals across a synapse (the gap between nerve cells).

Parkinson's disease: A progressive disease of the nervous system characterized by tremor, muscular rigidity, and slow, imprecise movement. It usually affects older adults.

Skeptic: A person who questions or doubts particular things.

hormones naturally make a person feel happier. The needles cause *asodilation* (increased blood flow), stimulation of **neurotransmitters**, and stimulation of the parasympathetic nervous system (sometimes called the "rest and digest" system). The easing of stress through acupuncture helps the *parasympathetic nervous system* and can lead to very deep relaxation. The system is a part of the body that can generate calm and give a sense of clarity. The parasympathetic nervous system is said to be an area of wisdom, for putting our experiences in perspective and seeing the "big picture."

Headaches Disappear

In 2012, scientists reported in the *Canadian Medical Association Journal* that migraine patients who received acupuncture showed long-lasting effects in the reduction of frequency and intensity of their headaches.

An in-depth look at the ancient healing art of acupuncture.

Reader's Digest presented the story of Karen Schwab in 2009. Twice a week she would get severe headaches that felt as if she were being stabbed in the head. First, she tried cutting certain foods from her diet (chocolate, caffeine, dairy) but the headaches continued. For 10 years, she took a prescription migraine medication, which offered some relief, but she grew tired of taking drugs.

To treat **migraines**, acupuncture needles may be put in the forehead, temple, face, neck, shoulders, hands, or feet. Schwab was nervous at first about the use of needles. (Just the word "puncture" can make some people anxious.) She admits that one feels the needles go in, but "they don't hurt." After a few weeks of therapy, her pain lowered to a mild pressure and the migraines never returned.

Many people who suffer migraines will take strong medicine to counteract the pain, but sometimes even that's not enough. Acupuncture is one alternative treatment.

Accupuncture-Related Therapies

There are a few twists on traditional acupuncture. With electroacpuncture a mild electric current is sent through the needles. Sonopuncture is carried out using a narrow, cylindrical high-frequency beam of sound instead of needles. With *fire acupuncture* (or *fired needling*) a heated needle is inserted. *Bee venom acupuncture* may be the strangest variation. This therapy requires injecting purified and diluted bee venom into acupoints. Bee venom has been shown to have properties that boost the immune system, increase white blood cell counts, and ease inflammation in nerve cells. It has eased symptoms for patients with **Parkinson's disease** and arthritis.

The chi and acupoints can be stimulated in other ways besides acupuncture:

• Acupressure replaces needles with different pressures and rhythms applied by the hands. Like acupuncture, it can reduce muscular tension, increase circulation, and enable deep relaxation.

• Moxibustion involves the burning of dried mugwort (moxa), a small, spongy herb, to help the healing process. In one approach, a small, cone-shaped amount of moxa is placed on top of an acupuncture point and burned. The patient experiences a heating sensation. Sometimes, the burning cone is allowed to heat the skin until it scars. In another approach, the moxa stick is lit and held at the acupuncture point until it turns red. In a combination with acupuncture, a needle can be inserted in the body, wrapped in moxa, and ignited. Heat is thus delivered to the acupressure point.

• Qigong does not involve pressure points but it does focus on helping the vital energy flow of the *qi* or chi. The qigong practices require posture (movement), breathing techniques, and mental focus. In some ways it is similar to yoga. The Qigong Institute in California says that qigong can be considered acupuncture without the needles because both practices involve manipulation and balancing of the body's energy.

• Reiki is a Japanese healing technique that uses touch to channel energy and restore physical and emotional well-being. The approach uses the palm of the hand on acupressure points, but no real pressure is involved—just light touch. This is a "laying of the hands" technique. Sometimes the hands can just hover above the body over the area where energy needs to be channeled, so there is no touching at all. Rei means "God's wisdom" and *ki* is the equivalent of "chi." The practitioner may say an internal prayer or affirmation to move aside the ego and let pure Reiki energy flow.

• Cupping therapy, like acupuncture, is an ancient form of therapy. One of the world's oldest medical documents, the *Ebers Papyrus,* describes how Egyptians used cupping therapy in 1550 BCE. The suction uses pressure to pull skin, tissue, and muscles upward. The thought is that this enhances circulation, relieves pain, and removes toxins. Recently, cupping therapy made headlines when Olympic gold medal-winning swimmer Michael Phelps used cupping,

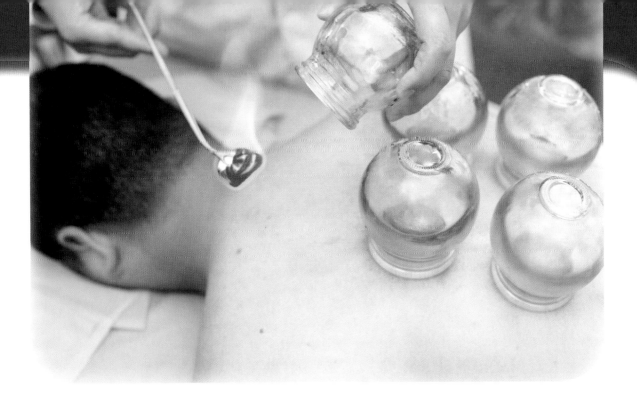

Although cupping has been around for centuries, it received renewed attention during the 2016 Olympic Games when Michael Phelps, and other swimmers were seen with large red circles on their backs and arms. These were effects of cupping.

leaving purple circular bruises on his body. (They are the equivalent of large hickeys.) Jennifer Aniston, Gwyneth Paltrow, Jessica Simpson, Lady Gaga, and Victoria Beckham are all fans of cupping. Traditionally, heated glass cups are placed at healing points along the body. The heat creates a suction and triggers an energy flow. There are two general approaches: dry cupping and wet cupping. Dry does not involve bleeding, and with wet, the skin is lanced and blood is allowed to flow. A 2012 review of 135 studies about cupping found that the practice had no benefit on sore muscles. Still, some scientists have said it could give a psychological boost.

CHAPTER 4

HEALING CRYSTALS

Healing crystals are used in a variety of cultures. Each stone or gem is believed to address specific ailments.

For thousands of years, certain cultures have believed that quartz crystals and gemstones hold healing energy. With crystal healing, gemstones are placed on the body, and they supposedly direct healing energy to flow in and negative destructive energy to flow out.

The practice goes back some 6,000 years. The ancient **Sumerians** used crystals in magic formulas, and the Egyptians used stones for protection and health. The Chinese valued jade as a healing stone for the kidneys. Aborigines of Australia, the Mauri people of Africa, and Native American tribes all used stones for spiritual and healing practices.

For example, amethyst, which is a type of quartz crystal with a purple coloring, gets its name from the Greek for "not intoxicated" and it was thought to protect against drunkenness and overindulgence. That's why ancient Greeks and Romans studded their wine goblets with these precious stones. Overall, amethyst is thought to chase away negative influence.

In the 1970s and '80s, Americans and other Western cultures became more interested in alternative approaches to medicine and healing, and a fascination with crystal therapy grew. The New Age minister Elizabeth Clare Prophet (1939–2009) described gems and crystals as **repositories** and transmitters of spiritual energy or light. The stones are used to relieve stress and pain, and some believe they can help with more serious ailments. Some crystal believers think certain gems can affect cancer. They see cancer as a blockage of energy and maintain that crystals can restore a proper energy flow.

Words to Understand

Chronic: Continuing for a long time; used to describe an illness or medical condition generally lasting longer than three months.

Repository: A place, receptacle, or structure where things are stored.

Resonate: To affect or appeal to someone in a personal or emotional way.

Sumerians: An ancient civilization/people (5400–1750 BCE) in the region known as Mesopotamia (modern day Iraq and Kuwait).

Scientific Take: The Stone-Cold Facts

Researchers call crystal healing a *pseudoscience*, meaning that there is little concrete proof to show that stones can actually heal or help health. However, some studies have shown that certain minerals may have healing effects. For example, a few investigations have observed

Famous "Stoners"

Victoria Beckham, Lena Dunham, and Katy Perry are among the top celebrities who swear by the power of stones. Katy Perry says that she sleeps with a rose quartz in her hand at night because it's supposed to help you find love and also heal your heart. Bethany Cosentino of the band Best Coast holds crystals in her hands while flying to feel less anxious. The singer/hip hop artist Raury carries crystals with him. He says that malachite helps him "stay grounded" and be a better communicator. Aragonite keeps him calm. On Complex.com, Raury said, "The thing about crystals and whatnot is that, just like your heart and your brain have electromagnetic waves, like brain waves, these crystals give off waves too, that **resonate** with your brain and your heart and are good for your health and well-being. Everything is vibrations. This whole thing about vibes and energy, it's not a hoax."

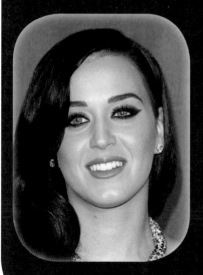  

Katy Perry, Lena Dunham, and Victoria Beckham all swear by the power of crystals.

that copper has an anti-inflammatory effect. Copper is utilized by almost every cell in the human body, and it has been used to treat **chronic** wounds, tuberculosis, burns, rheumatic fever, rheumatoid arthritis, sciatica, and seizures. Scientists also say that positive health effects may be achieved from the stones through a placebo effect. The process of using the stones also involves meditation, and this can help the body. Researchers emphasize that crystal healing should never be used to treat a life-threatening disease.

Some Top Rocks and Their Powers

Different gemstones are said by believers to affect different parts of the body (for example, green aventurine for the heart, yellow topaz for the mind).

Here are some crystals and gems and the healing properties associated with them:

- **Agate** is one of the oldest healing stones and is said to provide self-confidence and emotional strength. That's why it was used on protective breastplates in battle.

- **Bloodstone** is thought to detoxify the body, cleansing it of negative energy.

- **Blue lace agate** has been used to fight insomnia and get rid of headaches.

- **Citrine** is linked to building a stronger solar plexus.

- **Garnet** is said to help with depression.

- **Labradorite** (left) has the supposed ability to trigger the imagination.

- **Malachite** is thought to be good for the heart and throat.

- **Moonstone** is connected to hormone production and fertility.

- **Onyx** is used to fight melancholy.

- **Rutilated quartz** is said to speed healing and recovery.

Other Unique Healing Ideas

There are many types of healing therapies that are considered as alternative medicine. These are treatments that are not accepted by the world of traditional medicine. Here are a few memorable nonconventional health therapies:

Urine Therapy. Although there are no scientific data to support the practice, some believe that urine can be used for medicinal purposes. Devotees will drink their morning urine. Some prefer it straight and steaming hot; others mix it with juice or pour it over fruit! Believers say it helps counter just about every ailment—the flu, the common cold, broken bones, toothache, dry skin, psoriasis, snake bites, cancer, hypertension, and aging, to name a few. Urine advocates believe that pee has benefits outside the body as well. Madonna said her urine cured athlete's foot and the baseball player Moises Alou urinated on his hands to toughen them.

Leeches have been rediscovered by modern western medicine for situations as diverse as reconstructive plastic surgery and osteoarthritis.

Leeching. The medicinal use of bloodsucking leeches goes back to ancient Egypt. Bloodletting was once a cure-all remedy, but research has shown that the practice usually does more harm than good. Still, in some cases drawing off excess blood is helpful and leeches can be just the thing. For example, they can be a good option for safely removing congested blood from a wound. Leeches have also been used to treat nervous system abnormalities, dental problems, skin diseases, and infections. In addition, these worms secrete peptides and proteins that can help prevent blood clots. According to some reports, leech saliva may lower blood sugar levels and improve pancreas function.

The Miracle of Maggots. Ohio resident Pam Mitchell had a diabetes-related infection on both her feet that made it almost impossible for her to get around. She tried everything to treat the sores, but they kept getting progressively worse. Doctors put 600 live squirming maggots in the wound in her left foot and 400 in her right. The maggots helped remove dead tissue and expose healthy tissue in a process called *debridement*. At one point, doctors thought Mitchell might have to have her feet amputated, but the maggots cured her. Her feet healed and she was soon up and about, walking again.

- **Selenite** has been used by cancer patients for tumor reduction.

- **Turquoise** has been called "the master healer," used for overall body strengthening.

A documentary on healing crystals.

Gems Chase the Pain Away

In England, Kristy Hodges sold crystals and healing stones at New Age fairs. In 2013, she posted a story online about meeting a mother and daughter at one particular event. The mother, who was in a great deal of pain in her legs, was drawn to a large piece of malacholla (a natural, but rare combination of malachite and chrysocolla), which was full of copper sulfate. The woman bought a small piece. Hours later, Hodges received an excited call from her daughter—her mother was pain-free.

Another woman, from Nashville, TN, wrote online about her problems with lower back pain, and how the pain reached such levels of intensity that she could not sleep. The cycle of pain and sleepless nights led to depression. She visited a natural healer who had her lie on a table. The healer placed amethyst crystals on the woman's body and explained that they would open her *chakras* (centers of spiritual power in the human body). The chakra system originated in India between 1500 and 500 BCE. In Hinduism, a chakra is an energy point, and there are said to be seven main chakras running along the spine. After several sessions of relaxing with these gemstones, the woman felt her pain ease and she no longer needed antidepressants or sleeping pills.

The stone, malacholla.

CHAPTER 5

HYPNOSIS

Hypnosis is often known as a form of entertainment but there are some who turn to hypnosis for healing. Some use it to kick a bad habit, like smoking.

Hypnosis is a changed state of awareness. The word comes from the Greek *hypnos*, meaning "sleep." Under hypnosis, a person enters a trance-like state in which they are highly responsive to suggestion and direction. People under hypnosis are very relaxed and have a heightened imagination. Some describe it as a mental state between wakefulness and sleep. Believers say that it is a technique that can access the subconscious brain, so the subconscious can be reprogrammed. Hypnosis has been used successfully to treat pain, depression, anxiety, stress, habit disorders (like smoking, overeating), and many other psychological and medical problems. Some practitioners believe that it can be used to improve grades because it may reduce test anxiety, increase focus, and improve retention. People also use it to overcome self-defeating thoughts. The precuneus brain (which is involved in different aspects of consciousness) is still active under hypnosis.

I'll Put a Spell on You

While it is possible to hypnotize yourself (self-hypnosis), it's more common for a hypnotist or hypnotherapist to put someone into this state of consciousness. Some professional hypnotists seem to be able to use the technique to control people's wills. Performing hypnotists seem to be able to put people into an **automaton**-like state and then have them perform acts under their orders. The way a person acts under hypnosis, however, depends on how open they are to the process. To be hypno-

Words to Understand

Automaton: A person who acts in a mechanical, machine-like way; as if in a trance.

Mesmerize: To hold someone's attention so that he or she notices nothing else.

Precuneus: Part of the brain linked to episodic memory, visual-spatial abilities, and motor activity coordination strategies.

Sedate: Calm.

tized, the subject has to be in a relaxed state, which is usually achieved through dimmed lighting, deep breathing, and relaxation of muscles.

Talking in a low calm voice, the hypnotist suggests that the subject is getting sleepy and progressively achieving a very **sedate** state. Often the hypnotist will count down down from 10 or another number and say that when zero is reached, the person will be asleep and hypnotized. Some people are more susceptible to this type of suggestion. When an individual reaches this trance-like state, a hypnotherapist may make suggestions—perhaps to relieve pain or decrease stress and worry. Self-hypnosis is usually similar to meditation and is a way to relieve stress.

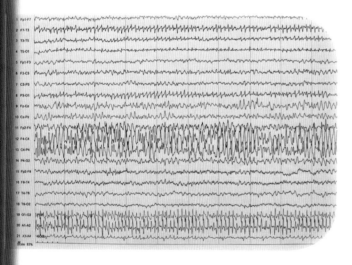

An EEG measures the electrical activity in the brain.

An inside look at the science of hypnosis.

Scientific Take

Under hypnosis, a person's heart rate and breathing slows down. Electroencephalograms (EEGs), which measure electrical activity in the brain, have shown that brain waves and electrical impulses in the brain change when a person is under hypnosis. Hypnotherapy has been shown to cure illnesses in some people—attributed to a mind-over-matter phenomenon. Some skeptics say that people who are hypnotized are merely acting that way—they are susceptible to pressure and the influence of others.

Past Life Regression

Some practitioners believe that hypnosis can be used to access memories of past lives and

Some advocates of hypnosis believe it can be used to access past lives or solve crimes.

incarnations. This tapping into previous lives is called *past life regression.* People reexperience episodes from their past lives. For some, the experience of these memories is sought simply out of curiosity, but for others, actions and attitudes in their past lives help them with their current life. These memories of past lives can reveal both positive and negative behaviors that people can draw upon to influence their current life. Sometimes, people can overcome negative behaviors that are holding them back.

Hypnotism to Solve Crimes

To solve crimes, detectives have occasionally used hypnosis on witnesses to help them recall essential facts. The process is called forensic hypnosis. The process was used to identify the famous serial killer Ted Bundy, who murdered at least 36 people. His final heinous act was the abduction and murder of a 12-year-old girl. There was only one eyewitness: Clarence Anderson. He thought he saw the abduction, but he could not remember details. Under hypnosis, however, Anderson was able to identify Ted Bundy as the murderer and his victim, Kimberly Leach. He even described their clothing. Skeptics, however, question whether memories under hypnosis are real or concocted. Some believe memories can be planted.

Mind Control Made Me Do It

In 1952, a 21-year-old American student, Girard Rosenblum, was found hanging in his basement. His death was ruled to be a suicide—at first. His family explained to a coroner's jury that Rosenblum was fascinated with the idea of achieving suspended animation through self-hypnosis. After reviewing the testimony and evidence, the jury agreed that his death was not a suicide but an accident resulting from "hypnotic research."

On March 29, 1951, 33-year-old Palle Wichmann Hardrup of Copenhagen walked into a bank with a gun and demanded money. When two workers resisted, he killed them both. Hardrup had a unique defense—he had been hypnotized by a cellmate while in prison and programmed to commit the crime. When the case went to trial, the cellmate, Bjorn Schouw Nielsen, was found guilty of planning the crime, and Hardrup was put in a mental institution, but the defense of hypnosis was not accepted.

One of the strangest cases of hypnosis gone awry happened in the spring of 2011 at North Port High School in North Port, FL. George Kenney, the school's principal, was using hypnosis to try to help students and staff perform better. He said he hypnotized about 75 people in total. He used his hypnosis techniques to try to help Marcus Freeman, the school's star quarterback, improve his game. But on March 16 of that year, Marcus drove a car off a road and died in a crash. His girlfriend said he had an odd look on his face before verging from the road. Kenney also hypnotized a student guitar player to help him as he was trying to get accepted to The Julliard School in New York City. That student, Wesley McKinley, hanged himself on April 8. The principal also tried hypnosis on Brittany Palumbo. She was suffering from test anxiety, and Kenney thought hypnosis would help. After five months of her grades not improving, she hanged herself in her bedroom closet. The principal was put on leave and eventually resigned. The school board awarded each family $200,000.

A Danish bank robber claimed he had been hypnotized by a former cellmate to commit the crime.

The success of stage hypnotists depends on volunteers who want to be hypnotized.

Stage Hypnosis

Many people are familiar with hypnosis from seeing performers who bring volunteers up from an audience and put them under a spell on stage. As with most hypnosis, the volunteers must want to be hypnotized for the spell to be effective. People who volunteer are not only more susceptible but more willing to do crazy things and help put on a show. They might act like a monkey or cluck like a chicken because they are natural show-offs, want to fit in, or have a tendency to help things go smoothly. One hypnotist tells his subjects that they will forget the number 2, and then has them count their fingers. One performer tells a volunteer that he will sing just like Elvis. Another makes people think they see dangerous snakes.

Mass Hypnosis

When hypnotist Maxime Nadeau performed before a group of 12- to 13-year-old girls at the Collège du Sacré-Coeur school in Sherbooke, Quebec, in June 2012, several girls in the audience were **mesmerized**. They went into a trance like state as well, and they had trouble coming out of the state. One girl was under the spell for five hours. The young hypnotist called his mentor for help and the students eventually returned to reality. The media called it a case of *mass hypnosis*. Mass or group hypnosis began with ancient civilizations. Many group rituals, such as mass chanting and meditation to a steady drum beat, were parts of religious "hypnotic" ceremonies.

Animal Hypnosis

The practice of hypnotizing animals has existed for centuries. French farmers were said to hypnotize their chickens to remain sitting on their eggs. One technique involved balancing wood shavings on their beak, which puts them in a trance-like state. Believers say cats, dogs, and cows can all be hypnotized. One technique is called *tonic immobility*. This involves physically restraining an animal, which then becomes immobile for a period of time.

Hypnosis in Novels, Movies, and Television
Hypnosis is a popular plot device. Here are a few memorable examples:

Dracula (1897). There is only one episode of hypnosis in the Bram Stoker novel— Dr. von Helsing hypnotizes a bite victim so she will reveal where Dracula sleeps during the day. In subsequent movie versions, Dracula uses the power of hypnosis to control people.

The Manchurian Candidate (1962). This film revolves around the idea that the Chinese hypnotized an American prisoner of war to return to the United States and assassinate the president.

Columbo (1975). In a memorable episode of this TV crime drama, the rumpled detective figures out that a woman's suicide was actually the result of a murder plot that included hypnosis. The victim jumps off a roof believing she is diving into a swimming pool.

Series Glossary

Affliction: Something that causes pain or suffering.

Afterlife: Life after death.

Anthropologist: A professional who studies the origin, development, and behavioral aspects of human beings and their societies, especially primitive societies.

Apparition: A ghost or ghostlike image of a person.

Archaeologist: A person who studies human history and prehistory through the excavation of sites and the analysis of artifacts and other physical remains found.

Automaton: A person who acts in a mechanical, machinelike way as if in trance.

Bipolar disorder: A mental condition marked by alternating periods of elation and depression.

Catatonic: To be in a daze or stupor.

Celestial: Relating to the sky or heavens.

Charlatan: A fraud.

Chronic: Continuing for a long time; used to describe an illness or medical condition generally lasting longer than three months.

Clairvoyant: A person who claims to have a supernatural ability to perceive events in the future or beyond normal sensory contact.

Cognition: The mental action or process of acquiring knowledge and understanding through thought, experience, and the senses.

Déjà vu: A sensation of experiencing something that has happened before when experienced for the first time.

Delirium: A disturbed state of mind characterized by confusion, disordered speech, and hallucinations.

Dementia: A chronic mental condition caused by brain disease or injury and characterized by memory disorders, personality changes, and impaired reasoning.

Dissociative: Related to a breakdown of mental function that normally operates smoothly, such as memory and consciousness. Dissociative identity disorder is a mental Trauma: A deeply distressing or disturbing experience.

Divine: Relating to God or a god.

Ecstatic: A person subject to mystical experiences.

Elation: Great happiness.

Electroencephalogram (EEG): A test that measures and records the electrical activity of the brain.

Endorphins: Hormones secreted within the brain and nervous system that trigger a positive feeling in the body.

ESP (extrasensory perception): An ability to communicate or understand outside of normal sensory capability, such as in telepathy and clairvoyance.

Euphoria: An intense state of happiness; elation.

Hallucinate: To experience a perception of something that seems real but is not actually present.

Immortal: Living forever.

Inhibition: A feeling that makes one self-conscious and unable to act in a relaxed and natural way.

Involuntary: Not subject to a person's control.

Karma: A Buddhist belief that whatever one does comes back—a person's actions can determine his or her reincarnation.

Levitate: To rise in the air by supernatural or magical power.

Malevolent: Evil.

Malignant: Likely to grow and spread in a fast and uncontrolled way that can cause death.

Mayhem: Chaos.

Mesmerize: To hold someone's attention so that he or she notices nothing else.

Mindfulness: A meditation practice for bringing one's attention to the internal and external experiences occurring in the present moment.

Monolith: A giant, single upright block of stone, especially as a monument.

Motivational: Designed to promote a willingness to do or achieve something.

Motor functions: Muscle and nerve acts that produce motion. Fine motor functions include writing and tying shoes; gross motor functions are large movements such as walking and kicking.

Mystics: People who have supernatural knowledge or experiences; they have a supposed insight into spirituality and mysteries transcending ordinary human knowledge.

Necromancy: An ability to summon and control things that are dead.

Neurological: Related to the nervous system or neurology (a branch of medicine concerning diseases and disorders of the nervous system).

Neuroplasticity: The ability of the brain to form and reorganize synaptic connections, especially in response to learning or experience, or following injury.

Neuroscientist: One who studies the nervous system

Neurotransmitters: Chemicals released by nerve fibers that transmit signals across a synapse (the gap between nerve cells).

Occult: Of or relating to secret knowledge of supernatural things.

Olfactory: Relating to the sense of smell.

Out-of-body experience: A sensation of being outside one's body, floating above and observing events, often when unconscious or clinically dead.

Papyrus: A material prepared in ancient Egypt from the pithy stem of a water plant, used to make sheets for writing or painting on, rope, sandals, and boats.

Paralysis: An inability to move or act.

Paranoid: Related to a mental condition involving intense anxious or fearful feelings and thoughts often related to persecution, threat, or conspiracy.

Paranormal: Beyond the realm of the normal; outside of commonplace scientific understanding.

Paraphysical: Not part of the physical word; often used in relation to supernatural occurrences.

Parapsychologist: A person who studies paranormal and psychic phenomena.

Parapsychology: Study of paranormal and psychic phenomena considered inexplicable in the world of traditional psychology.

Phobia: Extreme irrational fear.

Physiologist: A person who studies the workings of living systems.

Precognition: Foreknowledge of an event through some sort of ESP.

Premonition: A strong feeling that something is about to happen, especially something unpleasant.

Pseudoscience: Beliefs or practices that may appear scientific, but have not been proven by any scientific method.

Psychiatric: Related to mental illness or its treatment.

Psychic: Of or relating to the mind; often used to describe mental powers that science cannot explain.

Psychokinesis: The ability to move or manipulate objects using the mind alone.

Psychological: Related to the mental and emotional state of a person.

PTSD: Post-traumatic stress disorder is a mental health condition triggered by a terrifying event.

Repository: A place, receptacle, or structure where things are stored.

Resilient: Able to withstand or recover quickly from difficult conditions.

Resonate: To affect or appeal to someone in a personal or emotional way.

Schizophrenia: A severe mental disorder characterized by an abnormal grasp of reality; symptoms can include hallucinations and delusions.

Skeptic: A person who questions or doubts particular things.

Spectral: Ghostly.

Spiritualism: A religious movement that believes the spirits of the dead can communicate with the living.

Stimulus: Something that causes a reaction.

Subconscious: The part of the mind that we are not aware of but that influences our thoughts, feelings, and behaviors.

Sumerians: An ancient civilization/people (5400–1750 BCE) in the region known as Mesopotamia (modern day Iraq and Kuwait).

Synapse: A junction between two nerve cells.

Synthesize: To combine a number of things into a coherent whole.

Telekinesis: Another term for psychokinesis. The ability to move or manipulate objects using the mind alone.

Telepathy: Communication between people using the mind alone and none of the five senses.

Uncanny: Strange or mysterious.

Further Resources

Websites

Affiliation of Crystal Healing Organisations: *www.crystal-healing.org/*

This organization offers connections to many professional sources focused on crystal healing.

American Association of Acupuncture and Oriental Medicine: *www.medicalacupuncture.org/*

This group serves to advance the practice of acupuncture and oriental medicine.

American Cancer Society—Placebo Effect: *www.cancer.org/treatment/treatmentsandsideeffects/treatmenttypes/placebo-effect*

The ACS has a section devoted to the placebo effect, explaining how it does not cure disease but can relieve pain and other symptoms.

American Society of Clinical Hypnosis: *www.asch.net*

This society presents information regarding clinical hypnosis for health and mental health care professionals.

Applied Psychotherapy and Biofeedback: *www.aapb.org/i4a/pages/index.cfm?pageid=1*

An international society for mind-body research, health care, and education.

Movies

Here are some movies that feature alternative healing as a theme:

9000 Needles

The documentary follows Devin Dearth, a 40-year-old former bodybuilder, to China, where he is treated with acupuncture after suffering a massive stroke.

The Men Who Stare at Goats

A journalist heads to Iraq to investigate a Pentagon-funded project to harness New Age ideas to create jedi-monk-like super soldiers.

Further Reading

Bastarache, Rene. *The Everything Self-Hypnosis Book: Learn to Use Your Mental Power to Take Control of Your life.* Avon, MA: Adams Media, 2009.

Bauer, Matthew. *The Healing Power of Acupressure and Acupuncture.* New York: Penguin, 2015.

Birsche, Stephen. *Understanding Acupuncture.* Amsterdam: Churchill Livingston/Elsevier, 1999.

Blair, Forbes Robbins. Instant Self-Hypnosis: How to Hypnotize Yourself with Your Eyes Open. Naperville, IL: Sourcebooks, Inc., 2004.

Dispenza, Joe. *You Are the Placebo: Making Your Mind Matter.* Carlsbad, CA: Hay House, 2014.

Evans, Dylan. *Placebo: Mind Over Matter in Modern Medicine.* Oxford, UK: Oxford University Press, 2004.

Frazier, Karen. *Crystals for Healing: The Complete Reference Guide with over 200 Remedies for Mind, Heart & Soul.* Berkeley, CA: Althea Press, 2015.

Kenner, Corrine. *Crystals for Beginners: A Guide to Collecting & Using Stones & Crystals.* Woodbury, MN: Llewellyn Publications, 2011.

Robbins, Jim. *A Symphony in the Brain: The Evolution of the New Brain Wave Biofeedback.* New York: Grove Press, 2008.

About the Author

Don Rauf has written more than 30 nonfiction books, including *Killer Lipstick and Other Spy Gadgets, Simple Rules for Card Games, Psychology of Serial Killers: Historical Serial Killers, The French and Indian War, The Rise and Fall of the Ottoman Empire,* and *George Washington's Farewell Address.* He has contributed to the books *Weird Canada* and *American Inventions.* He lives in Seattle with his wife, Monique, and son, Leo.

Index